You Are Glorified

Let Everyone Consider

By

Bernard Benson Sarfo

Also by Bernard Benson Sarfo

The Fact Among Facts (1st)
The Fact Among Facts

Standalone
The Youth Murderer
Be Original Not a Copy
The Christians Science or Scholarship
Precious than Paradise
Habit Makes Future
A shelter from storm and rain
The Science of Life
The Strongest Lion Knockback
The Perfect and Inspiring City
Above Hope, Faith and Love
The Hero's Brave Decisions
The Weakest Among Plants
The Hero's Brave Decisions
Doing Above The Ability
The Wisdom Beyond Power And Greatness
Heavier Than the Heavens
The Academics Brains and Recreation Logics
The Strange Voice

The Chaotic World
Don't Miss Your Flight
Let the Nations Ponder
You Are Your Thoughts
I AM has sent me to you
Life Tools
The Fact Among Facts
You Are Glorified

Dedication

I dedicate this book to everyone in the world today and wish them salvation!

'When wisdom entered into your heart, and knowledge is pleasant unto your soul, discretion shall preserve you, understanding shall keep you' (Proverbs 2:10, 11).

Introduction

In Him was life and the life was the light of man. You need no other witness that Jesus die for you. He is alive to help and rescue those who will call for Him.

He is the one among thousands and the king among kings. He is the way; the truth and the life. There are cries everywhere on the globe.

People do not have peace; our ways are dark and evil every day. We are all dying and wailing; our hopes have gone and there is no help. Now is the time for you to seek God and live.

The whole world is in crisis and there is nothing that can helps or comforts us. It is time to seek God and live. He is the only solution to our problems. We need no other one; except Christ Jesus who dies on the cross for the entire world.

He is the one who can help and rescue us from this calamity which is in the world today. He is the one who the world need now and most. What have you considered?

What have you thought off? Will you accept Him as your personal savior? Why are you dying oh house of Israel? Seek Christ Jesus and live!

Whom shall we go to Lord? You are the one who have an everlasting word which we have believe and know that you are the holy God only son. Is there anyone who is near than you? Who can help us more than you?

Do not leave us or sake us, yet be our help and redeem us from our weakness. There are many things weighing us down. Our hope is gone and words are now lost. We do not know what to do and does not know where to go.

The world was created by Him. He is the author and finisher of everything. What are you searching for? Who do you need most or what man does the world need most? Why are you searching for things that profit nothing?

Is there anything that is necessary than Christ Jesus? What thing do you need that He lacks or cannot do for you? Who do you think He is or what have you thought of Him (Christ Jesus)? We must trust, believe and suffer for Him; then we will be glorifying with Him.

Contents

1. The Peak Act of God

Who can describe the beauty of God's love or who can explain to the deepest of God's attitude towards human beings?

Is there anything that is greater than the love of God? Who can totally understand the love of God? What is this love?

As the Owner and creator of the universe, He (God) creates an image resemblance to Himself and acting according to His likeness. God did everything that is needed for the image He made.

It is not by mistake but by intention to make someone live like Him. So, He formed the dust from the ground and made it like Himself and breathes the breath of life from His nostrils and that image He formed became a living being.

He taught him everything needed to be educating with and honored him more than the other creatures.

He (God) instructed him to trust His word to be obedient to that. The man owns everything, and he is the manager who controls and makes use of the surrounding creatures.

But he was forbidden eat from the tree in the midst of the place that the man lives. But man could not obey the words of God concerning not to eat from that tree.

The man distrusted the word of God and he did his wish but not what God wishes. But with all this stubbornness, God makes a way for man to live again and restored him to his office.

There was a death penalty for a man when he distrusts the word of God. It is a rightful way to get forgiveness of sin when the blood was poured.

So, God killed the lamb to make the man received the forgiveness of sin by His own love. The man was intentionally done wrong to God and distrusted His word.

But God with His mercy and love closed His eyes on it and forgave. How can we understand this love and what it is about?

Is there anything which can compare with God's love for us? Who can exchange his or her life for someone else? Or stand to die for somebody he does not know him and deserve to die for his sin?

We are sinners and deserve to die for the sins we have committed. Adam committed sin with his children and his children became sinners even when they are not yet born.

For all have sin and have fall short of the glory of God. (Romans 3:23). In fact, we deserve to die eternally because of the sin committed against God. Why because we insulted our Creator and distrust his words.

We have no excuse and have no answer to our sins. But God with His mercy and grace considered us again carried the sin to Himself as the one who has committed the sin and death for it.

This is the love of God for us given Jesus Christ to die for us. He was placed in our place as a sinner and die for it instead of us.

We cannot explain this kind of love and cannot know the reason of such love; because it is not possible for a master to die for a servant who has committed a grievous sin.

Or sleep outside for a servant to sleep in his bedroom for the sake of his own merit. I want you to know more about the love of God and His consideration towards us.

Who are we and what is our value? We are dust and are nothing to be used for something. How can we exchange a precious thing for a dust which cannot be used for anything?

With all our conditions, God did not look at it but considered and exchange His precious son for a dust (Man) or us. But God shows His love for us in that while we were still sinners, Christ died for us. (Romans 5:8).

Let us think of this statement and consider the question I am about to ask. One day a dog took somebody's meat and the man whose meat was taken by the dog pointed a gun on the dog and tempted to kill it.

But a setting man suddenly came and said kill me and leave the dog to go free. Instantly the man whose meat was stolen by the dog killed the man who devoted his life for the dog; and the dog fleet as was told by the devotee.

Everyone who heard was amaze about that incident. How can a man devoted to die for a dog? This is what Jesus did for us and there is no greatest love than this; that someone will die for his friends. In John 15: 13 says; Greater love has no one than this, that someone lay down his life for his friends.

Christ has redeemed us, by which we have no idea. We need to consider this act very carefully and be thankful every day.

God loves us so much that He exchanges His life for us. Moreover, there is nothing again that is needful in our life than his love for us.

We must think of it every day that He is ready for all our needs. We need not to fear of needs and do not worry about tomorrow. For if He did not spare his son but gave Him up for us, how can He freely not give us all things.

Who can condemn us? It is Christ who die for us and has risen from death and interceding for us. Let us read this text:

John 3:16 says;

("For God so loved the world, that he gave his only Son, that whoever believes in him should not perish but have eternal life)

Verse 17 says; For God did not send his Son into the world to condemn the world, but in order that the world might be saved through him.

Upon all our sins, God loves us and He has not condemned us. We are highly favored and esteemed by God.

It is God's will to be with Him in Paradise and stay eternally like Him! It is also God intention to be on earth again eternally as He did at the beginning. In fact, no one can explain the love of God towards us.

The love of God towards us cannot be explain by any language even Heaven Angel do not understand such a love.

God has make away by which we might have eternal life. All His doings are towards our salvation. It is God's will that none of us shall perish but to have eternal life.

Jesus wants us to live, and it is His will to die even eternally for us to live eternally! That is why He dies on the cross for our sins.

Let us consider this statement: our nature as human beings today is meaningless and it cannot be meaningful without Christ. We are not as what God wishes to work with; and we have lost the state that is meaningful to Him.

Our nature today has lost the glory of God and there is nothing with us that He can wish to make Him complete as God.

That is, we are not complete as to let God enjoy with us. We have totally lost His image and likeness. Means we have die to talk with by sin and have become useless more than first dust He used to create us.

We have been decay and corrupted by disobedient and there is nothing with us that makes God happy.

We are no more God likeness and image for His glory; we have been deformed by sin. But with all these conditions, God intended to restore and make us honorable again.

Moreover, there is nothing that can restore us to the first state, unless someone wishes to die eternally for us. And there is no one who can pay the price or redeem us from such a condition more worthy than the price! So, it's took God Himself to pay for it.

We have been redeemed by God's blood and it is His blood only that can pay the price but no other. How can we redeem by God's blood? Who are we? It's took God's life to makes our lives dear to Him. Means, there is nothing that can pay the price except God.

This is the love of God; it cost him to sacrifices Himself to make us well before Him! Oh my dear! What again do we need or what is our problem that God does not mind?

The amount of goodness which the whole human race can show to God cannot be anything concerning what God through Christ has done for us.

This is more than a precious thing or anything concerning treasured! We need not worry or think to lose our life unless we disregard God's love for us.

He has done everything which needs to be done for our salvation. Who are we that God love us so much? Let us read this scripture:

Romans 8:31-39.

What then shall we say to these things? If God is for us, who can be against us? He who did not spare his own Son but gave him up for us all, how will he not also with him graciously give us all things? Who shall bring any charge against God's elect? It is God who justifies.

Who is to condemn? Christ Jesus is the one who died—more than that, who was raised—who is at the right hand of God, who indeed is interceding for us.

Who shall separate us from the love of Christ? Shall tribulation, or distress, or persecution, or famine, or nakedness, or danger, or sword? As it is written,

"For your sake we are being killed all the day long; we are regarded as sheep to be slaughtered." No, in all these things we are more than conquerors through him who loved us.

For I am sure that neither death nor life, nor angels nor rulers, nor things present nor things to come, nor powers, nor height nor depth, nor anything else in all creation, will be able to separate us from the love of God in Christ Jesus our Lord.

We have no idea concerning this love and chance that God have shown to us. And we cannot answer, if we disregard this love of God. It will be a hell, if we dash this love on our foot. Means making this love of God a fruitless for our life! It is impossible for us to lose or separate from the love of God towards us, unless we make it void.

This is the inheritance of the children of God that no weapon can stand against us in judgment. Christ is the one who die for us. Who shall bring any charge against God's elect? It is God who justifies.

We have been given chance and opportunities likely to be accepted by God. There is no doubt about it our life is certain in Christ and has been sealed if we continue to make Him Lord in our life.

If we reject Him, He will reject us. If we embrace with Him, He will surely embrace with us. God is love and His love does not cease even when we are on our graves.

We dear to Him and shall be dear to Him eternally. He punishes us through His love and teaches us by His love.

What must we do or how shall we respond to His love towards us? Let us note this scripture in Hebrews 2:1-4, 8, 9 says;

Therefore we must pay much closer attention to what we have heard, lest we drift away from it. For since the message declared by angels proved to be reliable, and every transgression or disobedience received a just retribution, how shall we escape if we neglect such a great salvation?

It was declared at first by the Lord, and it was attested to us by those who heard, while God also bore witness by signs and wonders and various miracles and by gifts of the Holy Spirit distributed according to his will. Putting everything in subjection under his feet."

Now in putting everything in subjection to him, he left nothing outside his control. At present, we do not yet see everything in subjection to him.

But we see him who for a little while was made lower than the angels, namely Jesus, crowned with glory and honor because of the suffering of death, so that by the grace of God he might taste death for everyone.

Christ, taste death for us and there is nothing again that is more or greater than what He did for us.

He loves us even to death, for He wishes us to live by His death and wishes to die eternally for us even if He could not resurrected again. Have you imagined such a love before or are you now want to think off?

This is the love of God shown to us! We should not worry concerning what we will eat or cloth or sleep. Our situations are dear is to Him, and He will provide all our needs even if He must die for it.

Here, Christ paid the price by His blood to redeem us from the second death or the eternal death. He was killed for our sin penalty and has resurrected for all our needs. He is alive to advocate for us.

Isaiah 53:10 says: Yet it was the will of the Lord to crush him; he has put him to grief; when his soul makes an offering for guilt, he shall see his offspring; he shall prolong his days; the will of the Lord shall prosper in his hand.

We human beings sin against God at the beginning of our existence. We insulted our Creator and distrusted His words. The sin that was committed by our first parents was more than a curse.

This causes the unhealed decay to all human beings and there is no other thing that can solve this situation. But God took the cost to Himself, pay the price and bear the punishment.

Let us consider this act of God and cherish it! For He loves us and wants our wellbeing. Men let us love, for God is love! Note 1John 3:1-3 says:

See what kind of love the Father has given to us, that we should be called children of God; and so we are. The reason why the world does not know us is that it did not know him.

Beloved, we are God's children now, and what we will be has not yet appeared; but we know that when he appears we shall be like him, because we shall see him as he is. And everyone who thus hopes in him purifies himself as he is pure.

The love of God cannot cease and it is new every day great is His faithfulness. God has akin us to Himself and suffered for sin punishment for us. He bears the cross and shame for us and pays the price which no blood can pay for.

How must we respond to this love? We are His bride and everything He loves us and we are dear to Him even than Himself. Let us consider and do something that will show our appreciation towards what He has done to us!

2. The Great Service

It is very wonderful and difficult to understand God. It is not easy to describe the nature of God and understand His presence on earth.

His works are wonderful and very deep to discover. He is everywhere on the globe at the same time.

Can you imagine how things grow without seeing it with your naked eye? This is the Lord we serve; He above comparing or describing His being because no one has ever seen Him personally before. He is above everything but He is Humble.

Christ Jesus became flesh and lived among us. He took upon Himself human nature and became servant.

He disregards His nature as God and wish to be a servant for the sake man's life and dignity. Who can describe the love of Christ Jesus?

Who can tell reasons why He decides to die the unreturned or second death for a man? In fact, the highest and beauty of love and anything concerns love is to be selfless. It is the character surpasses character and everything called kind. It holds everything and there is nothing that can be comparing with. This is the nature and the attitude of Christ Jesus.

That is why all power has been given to Him by God and His name has been raise above all names both Heaven and earth. Who will die for thief or who will die for a murderer who deserves to die by his or her sin?

Jesus Christ accepted to die without remembrance for Adam and his children after him. The beauty of this attitude move God to raise His name above every name from Heaven to earth and under the earth. Who can be comparing with Him and who has ever done such before?

It is beyond good and what is called upright. Angels of do not understand the selfless nature Jesus Christ and they love to do what they can to support such a wonderful character to recue human race as did Christ Jesus wish.

That is why Christians are guided by Angels of Heaven. Christ Jesus is everything and He is above needs and wants of a man.

He sacrifices His life for no profit and die a second death without of hope of resurrection. He is dear son of God and only begotten son that whosoever believe in Him should not perish but have an everlasting life. Let's read

John 1:4, 5

In him was life, and that life was the light of all mankind. The light shines in the darkness, and the darkness has not overcome it.

He is the life and the light of all mankind. What must I say to you that you will believe Jesus Christ that I am writing about Him?

You can ask from end to the end of the world that there is no one who saves apart from Jesus Christ. Consider this text Acts 4:12 let's read:

Salvation is found in no one else, for there is no other name under heaven given to mankind by which we must be saved

Salvation is in no one else under the heaven given to mankind that we must be saved. Here Jesus Christ is the only who can save us from our sins and is He who God has accepted for us to be save through Him.

He is all in all and everything we need. He has done everything necessary for our salvation. He is our hope and has opened a way for us to be accepted and have our needs.

Read from Hebrews 4:16 Let us then approach God's throne of grace with confidence, so that we may receive mercy and find grace to help us in our time of need

We need not to worry about the matters of life but what must we be worry that our salvation is certain in Him?

Oh! What can I say again? The religious leaders cannot be our hope of salvation. They have no life in them and cannot be our hope. Do not trust anyone but Christ Jesus who is the resurrection and the life.

It is my hope that you will understand this message and do something about it. You need nothing but Christ Jesus who holds keys of death and the hades. He is your only hope of salvation and everything that you need. He is all in all.

3. The Water of Life

The source of life and every nature depend on this spring of waters to live. The world came out from waters and nature needs water to survive. In the beginning God created the Heavens and the Earth.

The earth was formless and empty. The whole face of the earth was covered with waters and deep. Darkness existed all over the earth and there was no dry land to be planted. The light was absent to see ahead.

But water has covered all the space of the ground. God commanded the light to appear and its came as He commanded. Why waters in everywhere in the face of the ground?

The firmament as we see are waters and the earth has been combined with waters. Water is life for the nature. That is all nature depends on water to survive.

There is a life in the water and the growth. The living things on this earth grow and survive by water. Without water nature and earth cannot survive. There will be no growth without water for the creatures. God put life in waters for nature to use and survive. We human beings cannot survive without water and light.

God did these two elements for our progress and comfortable life. The trees; grasses of the field, seeds and vegetables depend water for growth and life. Naturally, the world and things in it live by water.

The man became a living being when God breaths on his nostrils. We became a living being the breath of God. The living things as we see survive or live by water as we live by the breath of God.

Everyone must notice this message that I am giving out or sharing by God grace. We depend on something to have our being or live. Without that, we cannot survive or live as human beings.

Our life depends on someone to have our being. Who is it or who is our source of life? Many people think that they can survive each day and night with their own strength and it is max or automatic to live by your strength.

It is not so as they think. But there is someone who holds out our and make us lives every day and night. Who is that person?

It is Jesus Christ the son of God and only begotten who is in the bosom of the Father always make us live and have our being.

Never think that you own yourself and can do all things by your strength. Men, it is not so and cannot be anything without Him (Christ Jesus).

He is the life; the truth and the way. He is the fountain of the living waters that makes us alive day and night. Without Him, we will be nothing and cannot move or survive.

He is our source of life; the strength and the light. Without Him, there will no light; life and the living soul. We were nowhere and as nothing. We were dust which cannot be used for anything.

The world and the things on it were created by Him and it depends on Him to survive and have its beings.

As the living things like a tree cannot survive or grow without water; so, we human beings cannot survive or live without Jesus Christ our Lord and Savior. He is the fountain of the living waters.

Means, He is the all source of life and the life giver. In Him was life and the life was the light of men. He is the bread of life and the water of life. What can I say again? Let us note something from the Bible. Read;

Revelation 22:1

He showed me a river of water of life, clear as crystal, proceeding out of the throne of God and of the Lamb,

John 4:14 Read;

But whoever drinks the water I give them will never thirst. Indeed, the water I give them will become in them a spring of water welling up to eternal life.

There are a lot more that I can let you know but time will not permit me for more. He is the source of everything that we will be needed.

He is the life; He is the light, He is the water of life, He is the bread of life, He is the prince of peace and the everlasting Father.

It is Jesus; Immanuel. Our life depends on Him and without Him there will be no life. Whoever believe in Him and drink will survive eternally. Notice these Bibles texts and think about it. Read;

John 5:23 "Whoever does not honor the Son does not honor the Father who sent him."

John 5:42–43 "I know that you do not have the love of God within you. I have come in my Father's name, and you do not receive me."

John 6:45 "Everyone who has heard and learned from the Father comes to me."

John 8:19 "You know neither me nor my Father. If you knew me, you would know my Father also."

John 8:42 "If God were your Father, you would love me"

Will you consider and drink from the source of life? It is Jesus; your life, your way and the fountain of the living waters! No balm can heal you in this global disease, except the son of God who takes the sins of the world.

4. Our Substitute

God became human being and live amongst human beings. His name shall be called Immanuel; means God with us or God is with us. Who am I talking about? Who is that person lived among men but God Himself?

God ways are wonderful and difficult to understand His doings. Why did God live amongst us? What transpired? We committed sin at the beginning of our existence against God. It took God's life to solve this problem.

It became needed for God to turn into a man in order to restore His image and likeness that man has lost because of sin. The world turned into darkness because of the sin of Adam.

The case of Adam was so dangerous and perplexed. The whole idea of God to a man changed and rotted through the sin of Adam.

The joy of Heaven ceased at the moment and sons of God mourn about this incident. What will Heaven do about this episode?

The whole human race is at risk and the nature cannot live in peace for such situation. If there is a war, who must fight and lead? If the royal cease to fight, then servants will run.

The case became God case to fight for a man by His strength. This was not the hands and the cutlasses fight. But it is the war on sin. The war could not be a successful without the nature of a man.

Else, the war of sin cannot be a war for God. So, it took God to turn into a human being with flesh and blood as of Adam.

Here, God became second Adam and lived with flesh and blood. Who will wish to become a fish in the sea water and then live as a fish throughout his or her life last?

This is what Christ Jesus did for man sake. He became a man and lived amongst men with the same blood and flesh. Though, He is God but counted as no reputation to be equal with God.

He humbled Himself as a servant and became a man. His love is great and incomprehensive. He accepted to live as a man and fight the battle of sin. This is awesome decision and fabulous act. He won the battle on sin and has been honored with all power and the name above every name both Heaven and the earth and under the earth.

If God is for us, who can be against us? You should not worry and fear of wants. Why are you so fearful?

He (Jesus) has done it all and there is no other to be done again. He has finished the race for us and has fought and won the crown.

Read Romans 8:28-40

Read;

28And we know that in all things God works for the good of those who love him, whohave been called according to his purpose.

29For those God foreknew he also predestined to be conformed to the image of his Son, that he might be the firstborn among many brothers and sisters.

30And those he predestined, he also called; those he called, he also justified; those he justified, he also glorified.

31What, then, shall we say in response to these things? If God is for us, who can be against us? 32He who did not spare his own Son, but gave him up for us all—how will he not also, along with him, graciously give us all things?

33Who will bring any charge against those whom God has chosen? It is God who justifies. 34Who then is the one who condemns?

No one. Christ Jesus who died—more than that, who was raised to life—is at the right hand of God and is also interceding for us.

35Who shall separate us from the love of Christ? Shall trouble or hardship or persecution or famine or nakedness or danger or sword? 36As it is written:

"For your sake we face death all day long;
we are considered as sheep to be slaughtered."

[37]No, in all these things we are more than conquerors through him who loved us. [38]For I am convinced that neither death nor life, neither angels nor demons, neither the present nor the future, nor any powers,

[39]neither height nor depth, nor anything else in all creation, will be able to separate us from the love of God that is in Christ Jesus our Lord.

Is there anything that deceiving your heart? What are your longing for? What is your problem? What is difficult that Jesus Christ cannot be able to solve? What is the matter? He has accepted and died ready for your sake.

What again do you need for Him to do for you and accept Him as your savior and Lord? He is Immanuel; means God with us. He became a man and died for a man.

He is alive and advocate for us. Do not worry about your sins that you have committed, but confess to Him, He will have mercy on you and forgive all your sins. For He is alive forevermore and pleading for you.

He is merciful and gracious and abundant in goodness. What's your problem? He is Immanuel! He is with you and will not forsake you or leave you. Will you mind?

5. Why Are You wondering?

Sometimes life becomes hard and difficult to live. What shall I do about my situation? Where should I go to have relief? I do not know what to do? Can I survive in this condition?

These are your questions concerning your situation. But what have you observed about these conditions? Note: in all, you are still alive; you have not died yet. Have you asked that, why you are still alive?

Your circumstances and trials are your teachers guiding you to succeed. It is not there to destroy you, but it is building you to stand firmly.

In fact, bad conditions do not come to kill, but to make you alert and then prepare you for good management.

Do not wonder why it has happened to you. But learn to behave well in it. A calamity comes to prepare us for good works but not to wreck us.

Every bad situation has a purpose for us as human beings. Our condition has changed because of sin. So, it is good for us to suffer and to make a change. Do not wonder why? But ask for the reason and then make a change.

Do not lose hope, stop doubting and be at peace. It is not your doom but it is your welfare and correction.

Your life is not yours to make it the way you want it. But it is a choice and how you want by choice. One thing you should know is that it is God who directs your path and ends with your commitment.

Do not be afraid and never be discouraged. He knows the plans He has for you and thoughts that will make your success. Do not wonder or doubt about your situation.

He, who created the heavens and the earth, knows what are the best and good for you. He cares and shall not leave you alone to wonder. He, (God) allows trying times to come upon us and prepare us for good works.

It is not your duty to direct your path but you must allow God to direct it for you. You need to consider why you are still alive with all poverty and hopelessness situation. This means that you are loved and accepted by God. Be happy in all your condition, whether good or bad. Leave everything to God and stay at ease.

Your life is dear to Him and He will let you live in all your trials. God has seen you wondering, He is aware of that, He will do something about it. You should not stress yourself in the condition you cannot do anything about it.

Do not speculate, else you shall possibly lose your life. But be hopeful and knows that He (God) cares. This world was created for you, and you are the manager of those things that are in. what else do you need that is absent?

It is the sin of our first parents that has brought discomfort in life. But in all, it is for our aid and good to be in discomfort. Do not wonder; it is there for a moment, it shall come to pass.

Do not think that it is finished. Yet there is no hope again. Be hopeful, it is gone yet, but it is preparing you for your future crown. Are you wondering? Stop and be at peace. It shall be well.

6. Are You afraid?

Are you afraid? Are you discouraged? Do not be afraid? Do not be faithless? Maybe you do not believe God who created the heavens and the earth. It is the greatest sin to distrust God the heaven and earth creator.

Do not shorten the hands of God through you distrust of His word. What do you know about yourself? Do you know where you come from? If you do not know, then close your mouth. What do know about your life?

What can you do, if you do not know where you come from? Why are you fearful? Can you predict the end of your life? What do you know about the world and the creatures? Who feed the living ones and care for the non-living?

Do you have any idea? What can you say concerning the things of the world? Why are you challenging? Can you add one cubic to your height? Do you provide for the fishes in the sea? What is your burden?

What is weaning you down? Do you know the square meter of the earth? Can you measure the volume of the sea? Do you know the size of it? Did God has asked you to count all trees on the earth for Him? Do you know the density of this earth? Why are you afraid? Who is after you or chasing you? There is nothing to be fear in life and there is nothing that should border you.

Do not be afraid of anything but give thanks to God in all seasons. Do not make God small of your needs or do not short His hand through your disbelieve. You need not worry about anything.

Only let God hear your voice in prayer. He will take care of your problems and then solve them for you. As the child depends on his or her parents, so you should depend on God of your life. You need to trust Him.

Do not be afraid at all. Your problems are His problems. He is willing to provide and cares about your needs. He will not leave you to suffer for hunger. He will pour water on the dry ground and will make stream on the desert.

It is not your duty to be overwhelmed with many things. As you cannot do anything about day and night concerning this life matters.

So, you should stay calm and look to God. He is your provider in time of needs. Note: what Isaiah said concerning God's care for His children.

Read; 2"Enlarge the place of your tent, and let them stretch out the curtains of your dwellings; Do not spare; Lengthen your cords, and strengthen your stakes.

3For you shall expand to the right and to the left, and your descendants will inherit the nations, And make the desolate cities inhabited.

4"Do not fear, for you will not be ashamed; neither be disgraced, for you will not be put to shame; for you will forget the shame of your youth, and will not remember the reproach of your widowhood anymore.

5For your Maker is your husband, The LORD of hosts is His name; and your Redeemer is the Holy One of Israel; He is called the God of the whole earth. (Isaiah 54:2-5)

God is your husband and your redeemer. What is your problem? What He cannot provide for you? Is anything too hard for Him that He cannot do? He owns the Heavens and the earth. He is called the God of the whole earth.

Is there anything that He cannot do? Indeed, He can do all things. There is nothing that cannot worry Him or disturb Him.

You need not fear for wants or dismay about anything. Leave everything to Him and take heart. Disturb God by your prayers and let Him see your face every day and then hold your peace. Let nothing discourage you but keep on trust God about His words. He wants to hear your voice and you are dear to Him.

Consider this text; Ho! Everyone who thirsts, Come to the waters; and you who have no money, Come, buy and eat. Yes, come, buy wine and milk Without money and without price.

God is willing to give you anything you need. He will not request anything from you. You shall not pay for what He is giving to you.

It is free. He has seen your troubles and has seen your burdens. He is with you and cares. He is the God who sees and He has seen your trials. Note;

When you pass through the waters, I will be with you; And through the rivers, they shall not overflow you. When you walk through the fire, you shall not be burned, Nor shall the flame scorch you.

For I am the LORD your God, The Holy One of Israel, your Savior; I gave Egypt for your ransom, Ethiopia and Seba in your place.

Since you were precious in My sight, You have been honored, And I have loved you; Therefore I will give men for you, And people for your life. (Isaiah43:2-4)

We are not alone; God is with us. His name is Immanuel. He is with us in all situations. We are loved and honored. We have been ransom by Ethiopia and Seba. We have been protected by God.

All things work together for our good. There is nothing to fear or be afraid with. We need to trust God and be at peace. He cares and we are dear to Him.

Read;

But Zion said, "The LORD has forsaken me, and my Lord has forgotten me."

"Can a woman forget her nursing child, and not have compassion on the son of her womb? Surely they may forget, yet I will not forget you.

See, I have inscribed you on the palms of My hands; Your walls are continually before Me. Your sons shall make haste; your destroyers and those who laid you waste shall go away from you.

Lift up your eyes, look around and see; all these gather together and come to you. As I live," says the LORD, "You shall surely clothe yourselves with them all as an ornament, and bind them on you as a bride does. (Isaiah 49:14-18)

Do you afraid? Do not let the heart be troubled, believe in God and also in Christ. He is going to prepare a place for us and shall come back and take to Himself. Do not be afraid! He can do everything that is needed for this life and the life to come. Do you believe?

7. The Truth

Why I am writing something about what is the truth and who is the truth? Why truth? Many people are seeking for the truth but they could not find it yet.

Others too are asking what the truth is as did Palliate asked Jesus concerning truth. Why truth? What is truth stands for? Why do we need to seek for the truth?

If you will and wish to know the truth of the Bible, you will know and it will set you free. What is the truth and why do we need to search for it? Christ said; you shall know the truth and the truth shall set you free if you wish to know.

What is the truth? Why calling me Lord; Lord and do not what I say? The one who do the will of my Father shall know the truth.

Christ is the way; the truth and the life. So, if you really own Christ, you own the truth. Christ is the Law and the Law is the truth.

Everyone who keeps His commandment in him is the truth. The one who keeps the commandment and offense one is a liar. The truth is keeping the whole commandment of God and yet offense not one.

You cannot be a truthful by offended one of His commandment. The Law of God is truth and tester of the truth. To the Law and the testimony if they did not speak according to this; it is because there is no light in them.

So, Christ is the truth who is the Law of God. Everyone who live contrary to the Law of God, do not have the truth. For the one who have the son; has the Father and they will abide in him and they will manifest themselves to him.

Many Christians today has modified the way that leads to the truth. They have made their own way of worshiping God. Thinking that, you can choose anyway to worship God, it does not matter.

Do not deceive yourself, every act or worship will be tested by God's commandment, if it goes contrary to it, then it is not on truth.

The one who is the child of God does not sin, because His seed is in him and cannot commit sin, because he is the child of God. Everyone who does not do His will is a liar and does not have the truth in him.

The law of God is the standard of all truth and the tester of truth. Let's consider these texts from the Bible; read

<u>Psalms 119:165</u> [1]

Great peace have they that love Thy law, and nothing shall cause them to fall.

Psalms 119:142

Your righteousness is everlasting and your law is true.

John 17:17

Sanctify them through thy truth: thy word is truth.

If we live according to His word; not many or less but every word of God, then we have been sanctify by the truth; for His word is truth. Consider this text and listening to what the Bible is saying. James 2:1-12

2 My brethren, have not the faith of our Lord Jesus Christ, the Lord of glory, with respect of persons.

[2]For if there come unto your assembly a man with a gold ring, in goodly apparel, and there come in also a poor man in vile raiment;

[3]And ye have respect to him that weareth the gay clothing, and say unto him, Sit thou here in a good place; and say to the poor, Stand thou there, or sit here under my footstool:

[4]Are ye not then partial in yourselves, and are become judges of evil thoughts?

[5]Hearken, my beloved brethren, Hath not God chosen the poor of this world rich in faith, and heirs of the kingdom which he hath promised to them that love him?

[6]But ye have despised the poor. Do not rich men oppress you, and draw you before the judgment seats?

1.　　https://www.biblestudytools.com/tmba/psalms/119-165.html

[7]Do not they blaspheme that worthy name by the which ye are called?

[8]If ye fulfill the royal law according to the scripture, Thou shalt love thy neighbour as thyself, ye do well:

[9]But if ye have respect to persons, ye commit sin, and are convinced of the law as transgressors.

[10]For whosoever shall keep the whole law, and yet offend in one point, he is guilty of all.

[11]For he that said, Do not commit adultery, said also, Do not kill. Now if thou commit no adultery, yet if thou kill, thou art become a transgressor of the law.

[12]So speak ye, and so do, as they that shall be judged by the law of liberty.

Here the Bible makes it clear that the truth is doing what the word is saying to you. This is the truth. If we do away one word of His words, then we are not in the truth.

But walking outside of the truth: Note 3 John 1:4 read;I have no greater joy than to hear that my children walk in the truth.

The word of God is the truth and that word is Christ Jesus. He is the truth; the way and the life. Many Christians wants to choose some of the words and leave all the rest for their own selfish life.

They come near with their mouth but their hearts are far away concerning the truth. That is, they want to do their own will but not the will of God.

They have big title like right reverend and so on but not in the truth. They have chosen their own way of worship and living as they wish.

My dear, I want you to know and keep in mind that, if you reject single word or jot or comma or dot in the Law of God, then you reject God and you are not in the truth. The truth is living as His word has commanded you. If you want to do His will, then you will know the truth concerning Him. Many people are seeking for the truth whiles they reject to do His will.

So, the truth is saying and doing what His words are commanding you to do. In this that we know we are in the truth by doing what His word is commanding us. The truth is the love and the love is the truth. The love is His commandment and the commandment is His love and truth.

We cannot be truthful whiles we reject to do all His commandments. The truth is keeping the Law by His grace. For you shall know the truth and the truth shall set you free.

Means you will have peace by keeping His (God) Law but not as a Law breaker; because great peace have those who keep His Law and nothing offense them.

This is what concerning truth and the truth that we live according to His words. Note: everyone will face judgment according to his or her doings but those who keep all His words will be free from doom. Read; Revelation 14:12; Here is the patience of the saints: here are they that keep the commandments of God, and the faith of Jesus. The truth is Christ Jesus! Do you believe? Then you will be set free by having faith in Him.

8. The Answer

Our hope has been certain in Christ. The cry and the worry of John the revelator have been answered. John the revelator cried in his dream when he couldn't found the one who is worthy to open the seven seals of God for the destiny of mankind certainly established.

The whole world is in trouble; the time is coming where no one can survive comfortably. Our destiny has a question that needs the answer. Sin has changed the direction of our life. We are all in trouble and yet the questions to be solve.

Who can stand and answer these question that concerning life and death? Oh world! There is a case on it way coming.

The world needs to be destroying and rebuilt again by God. But there must be a remnant that needs to be establishing again to God for eternity.

This cannot be done, unless the seal of God that holds this world destiny open by someone; not just anyone but the one who is worthy. The worthy one should not be an Angel of Heaven who knew no sin. But a man likes Adam who is blameless and has lived in the world with flesh and blood but without fault or anything that is called sin.

That person is the only one worthy to open the seal of God for the world to have its proper cloth again. The penalty of sin cannot be solved by Angels of Heaven. It needs a man to solve it for a man. He has been glorified and highly lifted!

Jesus Christ accepted this condition and became a man to solve man's problem. He became a man with all sorts of trials that leads a man into sin. But He stand firm with no sin and committed all His case and everything to God.

He was accuse and persecuted by men. He faced all circumstance that leads to sin, but He did not sin. He was accuse with false pretends and the end nailed Him on the cross.

With all sorts of accusation, He closed His mouth as a sheep in the hands of a slaughter. He did this for the sake of a man.

Who can explain this kind of act that Jesus revealed in His life? He made it for the sake of mankind. He was rejected by a man for the sake of a man. He was pears by a man for the sake of a man. He nailed to the cross by a man for the sake of a man.

He did all for a man to be restoring again. It came to pass, John the revelator cried in his dream for he did not find the one who is worthy to open the scroll of the seals of God for the sake of a man.

Every good and precious thing did not talk but those that are good for nothing talks a lot. Jesus waited and delayed a bit to see what will John the revelator will do.

He shake his faith to see if John the revelator still believe that He (Christ Jesus is and is able to open the scroll of the seals for man assure of his salvation.

One of the elders in John's dream told him to cease cry, because the lion of Judah the seed of David is worthy to open the scroll of the seals for man salvation reassured.

Christ Jesus is worthy to open the scroll of the seals of God. He died and alive and holds the keys of death and hades. He has bought us with His blood and He is alive forever more to advocate for us.

Jesus is our only hope for salvation. There is no other thing or a person needed to be saved through him. Our good works cannot save us; our love shown to others cannot save us.

There is nothing but Christ Jesus can save us. It is He only but not the other. He is worthy to open the scroll and lose the seven seals of God. Let's read the Bible and think of the seals and the one who is worthy to open and lose it. Read;

Revelation 5:1-14

Then I saw in the right hand of him who sat on the throne a scroll with writing on both sides and sealed with seven seals. [2]And I saw a mighty angel proclaiming in a loud voice, "Who is worthy to break the seals and open the scroll?"

[3]But no one in heaven or on earth or under the earth could open the scroll or even look inside it. [4]I wept and wept because no one was found who was worthy to open the scroll or look inside.

[5]Then one of the elders said to me, "Do not weep! See, the Lion of the tribe of Judah, the Root of David, has triumphed. He is able to open the scroll and its seven seals."

[6]Then I saw a Lamb, looking as if it had been slain, standing at the center of the throne, encircled by the four living creatures and the elders. The Lamb had seven horns and seven eyes, which are the seven spiritsof God sent out into all the earth.

[7]He went and took the scroll from the right hand of him who sat on the throne. [8]And when he had taken it, the four living creatures and the twenty-four elders fell down before the Lamb. Each one had a harp and they were holding golden bowls full of incense, which are the prayers of God's people.

[9]And they sang a new song, saying: "You are worthy to take the scroll and to open its seals, because you were slain, and with your blood you purchased for God persons from every tribe and language and people and nation. [10]You have made them to be a kingdom and priests to serve our God, and they will reignon the earth."

[11]Then I looked and heard the voice of many angels, numbering thousands upon thousands, and ten thousand times ten thousand. They encircled the throne and the living creatures and the elders.

[12]In a loud voice they were saying: "Worthy is the Lamb, who was slain to receive power and wealth and wisdom and strength and honor and glory and praise!"

[13]Then I heard every creature in heaven and on earth and under the earth and on the sea, and all that is in them, saying:

"To him who sits on the throne and to the Lamb

be praise and honor and glory and power,

for ever and ever!"

[14]The four living creatures said, "Amen," and the elders fell down and worshiped.

Jesus has done it all and our hope has been curtained. My dear! Let's consider this act of Christ Jesus and do something about it. He is worthy and accepted by God for us to be considering again. What is the seal and what is it about? Read some of it: Revelation 7:1-3

After this I saw four angels standing at the four corners of the earth, holding back the four winds of the earth to prevent any wind from blowing on the land or on the sea or on any tree.

[2]Then I saw another angel coming up from the east, having the seal of the living God. He called out in a loud voice to the four angels who had been given power to harm the land and the sea: [3]"Do not harm the land or the sea or the trees until we put a seal on the foreheads of the servants of our God."

Let us notice some event in it in Revelation 8:1-13.

Read;

When the Lamb opened the seventh seal, there was silence in heaven for about half an hour. [2]Then I saw the seven angels who stand before God, and seven trumpets were given to them.

[3]And another angel came and stood at the altar with a golden censer, and he was given much incense to offer with the prayers of all the saints on the golden altar before the throne, [4]and the smoke of the incense, with the prayers of the saints, rose before God from the hand of the angel.

[5]Then the angel took the censer and filled it with fire from the altar and threw it on the earth, and there were peals of thunder, rumblings,flashes of lightning, and an earthquake.

[6]Now the seven angels who had the seven trumpets prepared to blow them.

[7]The first angel blew his trumpet, and there followed hail and fire, mixed with blood, and these were thrown upon the earth. And a third of the earth was burned up, and a third of the trees were burned up, and all green grass was burned up.

[8]The second angel blew his trumpet, and something like a great mountain, burning with fire, was thrown into the sea, and a third of the sea became blood. [9]A third of the living creatures in the sea died, and a third of the ships were destroyed.

[10]The third angel blew his trumpet, and a great star fell from heaven, blazing like a torch, and it fell on a third of the rivers and on the springs of water. [11]The name of the star is Wormwood.

A third of the waters became wormwood, and many people died from the water, because it had been made bitter.

[12]The fourth angel blew his trumpet, and a third of the sun was struck, and a third of the moon, and a third of the stars, so that a third of their light might be darkened, and a third of the day might be kept from shining, and likewise a third of the night.

[13]Then I looked, and I heard an eagle crying with a loud voice as it flew directly overhead, "Woe, woe, woe to those who dwell on the earth, at the blasts of the other trumpets that the three angels are about to blow!"

We need not to fear or shake for what is about to happening in our world. But we need to do something, and what is that thing? If you are not truly the follower of Jesus, then decide now and accept and follow

Him. That is what you need to do. He is worthy to open the book and break its seals for your sake. Will you consider? It's Jesus!

9. We Have No Idea

Have you ever ask yourself concerning your existence as human being and not the other creatures? Have you thought of why you are here on earth?

In fact, we have no idea concerning our existence and we cannot tell how we came about. But there is a reason why we are here on earth. Everyone has the duty and reason why we are here on earth. Let's read this scripture:

Jeremiah 1: 4, 5

Now the word of the Lord came to me, saying,

"Before I formed you in the womb I knew you,

and before you were born I consecrated you;

I appointed you a prophet to the nations."

Do you have an idea concerning our lives today on earth, but there is a purpose for us to complete or accomplish?

God appointed us for a duty. It is not a mistake to be here on earth, but there is a reason. Have you asked yourself concerning the work that God has appointed you to accomplish?

What is your work now and how do you do it? What is the benefit that your work is providing?

Are you honest to the work that you have been appointed? Are you selfish? How do others recognize you about your work that you are doing? How serious are you?

In fact, we are appointed by God to work for Him but not ourselves. Everyone needs to take note concerning the reason why we are alive today on earth.

Why are we here? We are here for a purpose and a duty that needs completion. Many people think that they are here only for fun and selfishness. You are glorified and honored for your life today.

Some also consider life as has no reason but live as you wish. Jeremiah was appointed to be the prophet for nations; to pull down and build.

Means to prepare people for God and make stand perfectly before Him. It is not by accident that you are here on earth but you have been appointed for a duty.

Never live as useless being or live as you own yourself and can do whatever you wish. It is not so, but God has appointed you to work for Him concerning other people's progress. God wants you to prepare others for Him through your gift and make others survive through the work that you are doing.

Do not work as you are working for yourself but work as you have been appointed for. We are here to fulfill the mission of the owner of creation but not as we want it to be.

It is a mistake to live and work for selfish living. Many people fail concerning life matters and misuse their time for no sacrifice for others benefit.

Others abuse their gift for no improvement and die for no history activities. Do not live without good name and do not die without history of your good activities on earth.

Else, you have failed to be recognized absolutely on the new earth. Everyone needs to work according to as he or she has been appointed.

Never live as without responsibility or goal but make your living meets its target. We were appointed even before been in the womb of our parents. And we were consecrated and knew by God before we were born. We are to use our talent or gift to fulfill the mission appointed by God.

Many people do not know that they have been appointed to do some specific job purposely for their fame. Others do not consider their gifts as precious but bury them through less recognition.

In fact, we cannot be anything if we put aside our gifts without using it. And it is good that we were not born than to be born for not using our gifts for owner's mission. Our mission is to fulfilling the mission of the owner through our gifts.

Moses was afraid to lead Israelites from bondage when he was appointed by God. He tried to ignore the journey to redeem Israelites from Egypt, but God instructed him to fulfill his plan.

This is the purpose of God and the purpose was to fulfill by Moses. Here Moses does not that God has appointed him to fulfill His mission before he was born. It was God's intention, but not by accident or chance.

Our talent goes with our mission and it has been planned by God not by chance but corresponding to our ability. So, we are not here as useless beings but useful beings and important managers. Our mission does not matter the age; whether child, youth or elderly.

Our goal is to fulfill the mission as soon as the life begins as human beings. Our life develops through the stages of mission progression.

We should not work according to the age but should work according to the purpose set up before us.

Means we will develop through using our talents and then make differences through the age development. This makes us work perfectly and beautifully for the Master. Let's consider this scripture:

Jeremiah 1: 6-8

Then I said, "Ah, Lord God! Behold, I do not know how to speak, for I am only a youth." But the Lord said to me, "Do not say, 'I am only a youth'; for to all to whom I send you, you shall go, and whatever I command you, you shall speak. Do not be afraid of them, for I am with you to deliver you, declares the Lord."

Here, we are to be alert for the Master's mission and not to complaining about our incapability. Our duty is to accomplish the mission of the Master. Let everyone make use of his or her gift for the glory of God.

King Cyrus was appointed by God before he was born to fulfill God's mission in his time. Everyone has been appointed to work for God. We are not here just to make the earth fill with people but to work for the Master who created us.

Let's read from Isaiah 45:1- 7

Thus says the Lord to his anointed, to Cyrus, whose right hand I have grasped, to subdue nations before him and to lose the belts of kings, to open doors before him that gates may not be closed:

"I will go before you and level the exalted places, I will break in pieces the doors of bronze and cut through the bars of iron, I will give you the treasures of darkness and the hoards in secret places, that you may know that it is I, the Lord, the God of Israel, who call you by your name.

For the sake of my servant Jacob, and Israel my chosen, I call you by your name; I name you, though you do not know me.

I am the Lord, and there is no other, besides me there is no God; I equip you, though you do not know me that people may know, from the rising of the sun and from the west, that there is none besides me; I am the Lord, and there is no other.

I form light and create darkness; I make well-being and create calamity; I am the Lord, who does all these things.

God has appointed us to work for Him but not for ourselves. It is God's plan for us to be here on earth but not accident or chance. Everyone must fulfill this mission and fulfill the Master's purpose for our lives.

We are here to see God who created the heavens and earth to share the beauty of His glory. We have been invited and honored to be on earth.

We were nowhere to be found or existed. We were created from dust without hope and life. We are like dead tree or nothing to be considered. But God with His mercy and consideration with grace make us His own likeness and image.

God wants us to work with Him and join us to be in His Company as His coworkers. So, it is not our will or desire to be called by God. But it is His wish and plan to let us be in His Company as His coworkers. We have no idea and we were nothing to be recognized. So, it is not you but God who intends to make you to be with Him.

You have no word to say and have nothing to share with Him. It is His consideration and love but not beauty or anything concerning us.

Who are we to get such an opportunity to be with or called or created by God? Who can say what are you doing or question God concerning His activities?

We were created for a reason but not for anything. Everyone has work to do for the Master. We need to watch out and be careful by the way we do things.

We need to be considerate and work for the Master. We must be ready and prepare ourselves for the Master's call. Let us consider this Scripture:

Ezra 7: 10 say;

For Ezra had set his heart to study the Law of the Lord, and to do it and to teach his statutes and rules in Israel.

We have work to do and have a duty to perform. There are no reasons to question the Master or our Creator concerning our work or duty that needs accomplishment.

We are His image and likeness created for His glory. We are His coworkers and loved through His mercy and grace.

We are here not to be idle but to work and progress in life. We are to work and live daily for God but not for any reason that we supposed to work for. There is no question to ask unless you do not know or maybe you need to understand some setting things.

Everyone must find out his or her talent makes use of it. We should not be useless beings but useful beings because we have the tool to work with.

It is not God's plan to create a useless thing in His creation and it has been never His plan to create something that has no duty to perform or useless thing in His creation. Note this scripture:

Proverbs 16: 4 say;

The Lord has made everything for its purpose,

even the wicked for the day of trouble.

Everything that is visible or invisible has a purpose and the reason it was created. We need to understand and know that there are no useless creatures, but useful ones and important for us to make use of it as human beings.

We have been privileged enough and honored to be His glory. Why we are here needs your attention to live and work for God. For you were created for His glory and praise.

Note: Isaiah 43:4, 7 says: Because you are precious in my eyes, and honored, and I love you, I give men in return for you, peoples in exchange for your life. everyone who is called by my name, whom I created for my glory, whom I formed and made."

We were created for His glory and honored. We need to fulfill our missions and glorify God who created us.

Why are you here? We are here for a reason or purpose and it needs fulfillment. What are you doing to fulfill your goal but not as useless beings?

10. What Is Next?

Every tree that is planted bears fruit. So, is the every deed proceeding? Everyone is going to receive his or her reward through the performance revealed. We have rewards with the Master which is equal to the deeds.

What are you going to receive when the Master comes? It is not all when you die, but there is a judgment. Everyone is going to receive his or her price when turns to him or her according to the work done.

Whatever you do, you will be harvested. Great men are not always wise, nor do the aged always understand justice. Do not consider yourself as the mighty, yet be humble and know the time.

But there is a spirit in a man, and the breath of the Almighty that gives him understanding. Whatever the case, everyone is going to face the fruit of his or her deeds. Someone will say or ask, if you die, is it all? Or is there anything again after death?

What do I mean about this content? What will happen after? The Bible has made it clear that there is a judgment after death. If there is judgment, then there will be resurrection. This death that we see is a first death, and also it is a sleep. The time is coming when everyone will be rise from the death.

Those who believe God and accept Jesus Christ as their personal savior will be resurrected when He comes in the second time. Those who did not accept Him would be dead with those who are already dead for thousand years.

When the thousand years are over, Christ will come on this earth again with the saints who had life at His second return with the Holy City (The New Jerusalem) to this earth. Those who did not receive their share at His second return will have their reward after the thousand years.

Here, the fire will come down from Heaven and then consume them. This will be the reward of those who did not have chance to enter Heaven within the second coming of Christ. Here, Christ will pay the wicked according to their deeds by fire and brimstone.

There is a reward for every deeds or work. So, this life is not all, yet there will be reward. What have you considered? Do you respect? What are your deeds?

The world will receive it due by it deeds. Do not deceive yourself and never make yourself light whiles you are dark. Do not pretend to be good, whiles you know it is not so. Stop pretending and then do things right and according.

We all have case with the Master. If you look around what do you see? What is going on? What are you doing? What is your share? How do you do your things? This is not all, yet there will be a reward for each deed.

Many people think that there would be no judgment after this life. Others also think that this life is all, there is nothing again. Do not joke of this life and never waste your time on things that are not necessary.

You need to consider yourself well and then do things right. This life is not all, yet there is another thing after this. Do not be wise at your own estimation to destroy yourself. But consider the outcome and then behave well.

This life is not all, yet there is judgment which nothing can be compared. My dear, we have case with the Master, so know how to behave and then do things according to the requirements. There is judgment and reward after this life.

11. Learning Something

The world is the lesson field which involves so many subjects and objects. We are subjected with so many lessons and the reasons to live in the world. The question is why?

There are so many penalties and problems in the world. Evil spirits are all over the world fighting against us physically and spiritually. They are the sources of the world problems and a wreck of human's life.

We are in danger in every moment which needs consideration of act we expose at each day. The journey of Israelites in the wilderness for forty years was an example for Christian's journey to Heaven today.

It is a journey of war against principalities and the forces of darkness. Whatever happened to them will happening to us through this journey we are in today.

Their test at that time is our test today which signifies the beauty of this journey. Our life is dear to God and He wishes our best of life. It is His wish to make us dear again.

Whatever comes our way is His permission for our progress. He loves us and wishes us best and great future. We should not get annoyed when we hate by any danger.

Yet all things work together for our good and progress. The circumstances in our life are our guides which make us strong through this journey of life and its best.

It is the food that sustains the life growth for the best gains. It is not there to harm or kill us, but to boost us and opens our eyes for best steps making. The lessons of life are the teachers of life and the knowledge that gives us correct understanding through our life journey.

The heat that you are passing through will not burns you, but yet to let the sins go and then free you for pure growth that the King demands. We are to achieve best reward which is the life gold that suits the highest stage.

We need to learn more from this life as did Israelites walked in the wilderness for forty years. Whoever wishes to be a Heaven representative will face terrible trials on this earth.

This is not the destiny of the saints but for purification of the character that fits the Heaven one.

Our life on this earth has encountered so many stains of sins and it needs to be purifying by circumstances.

Many of us mind has been bought by food and money. This attitude cannot meet the requirements that needs on the Promised Land. Some of us are faithless and timid.

Others love food than life. These are the things that prolong the journey to the Promised Land. The new house needs new goods and new stuff for decoration.

The old nature that has encountered so many stains needs to be prepared and dress with the new one to fit the fresh one. The children of Israel faced scarcity of food and water through their journey into the Promised Land.

They were tested concerning that to proof their faith in God the Almighty. Yet many of them failed for lack of faith and then stumble on the way. Sometime many of us think that, the food is all about life. But that is very wrong!

We are not here on this earth because of food, shelter and so on. That is not God's purpose or intention, yet He wants us to be free and then be like Him.

Many of us lack faith and then fear of wants. The life must sometimes face scarcity of things needed for development. If it were not so, no one will fully meet the will of God that brings eternal life.

The world is full of evil spirits fighting against our progress and our eternal life. Mistakes and other circumstances are our chief teachers teaching us on carefulness.

God permit trials to build us strong and then make us on track sometimes. Let us understand that, material things can steal and then make us lost eternally.

The journey made by the children of Israel in the wilderness for forty years is an example of life matters that every correct Christian must face. Our hearts and minds needs to repent from unrighteousness.

We are rebellion children like the Israelites which resulted their long years in the wilderness. So, trials were permit to let them change from their bad behavior.

As Christians, we will face many trials like them, not to harm us but to bring us on track. We should not worry as the strange thing that has happened to us.

Yet, we must take heart and then be at peace. The promise for us is, I will not leave you nor forsake you! Let us note that, our life is dear to God and He wants us to be like Him and then live with Him.

12. The Purpose of Life

Life is not about money that we seek for each day. It is not like gold that we refine for precious things. Yet, it is a daily practice that needs improvement throughout eternity.

The activities and the actions are the witnesses about the good or bad life we demonstrate each day. What must you know concerning the eternal life? Life is everything concerning world we live.

When life is out, then there is no world or reality. If there is something that needs first and bigger consideration, it is life! The only need that man must seek is life.

As human beings, we must put everything aside and then seek for life first. How must we seek for this life I am talking about? In Him was a life and the life was the light of a man.

He is the resurrection and the life. He is the way, the truth and the life. Many of us are seeking for the properties of the world. Others are seeking for luxuries of this world.

What is the benefit of these things when there is no life? Can you seek for food when you do not have life? Why are you seeking for dead thing instead of life thing? As you cannot build a house without proper preparation, so you cannot make life without life source.

The children of Israel seek for food instead of life and good character. We cannot live without the life giver. So, we must live the life with the life giver.

Everyone must seek the life and it giver before anything else concerning that. We fail of correct attitude as human beings because of sinful nature we have. Many of the children of Israel died for the lack of faith.

The entire children of Israel who began the journey early died on the wilderness because of rebellion. Life is not about food, clothing and shelter. It is about wellbeing that consists of eternal life.

We must consider our attitude and behavior in our entire move. Life is to seek the kingdom of God and it righteousness and all things will be added unto you.

Let everyone consider his or her behavior and then seek for the treasure or pearl of life. The key is that, let all of us seek for the life giver or the master of life. We should avoid those weeds and then seek for the seed. The world and the things in it are for the Lord.

Whatever we see is from Him. Do not let the things of the world take you captive, yet seek the Kingdom of God and it righteousness, then all things will be yours. Means all things will work together for your good.

Let not your heart be trouble, believe in God and move. You cannot always get it right as you wish; but note that, all things will work together for your profit.

In all, mind your business and then fear God! Do not rush and do not do things for granted, else you will fail. The children Israel failed, because of unbelief and distrust.

They thought of flesh, instead of reasoning about their life purpose. Many of them perished in the wilderness and then could not reach the Promised Land. Let us make the most of our time and then keep watch. We will receive the crown.

13. I Am Weak

In fact, I cannot do for myself and I do not know how to do it. It is not my fault; I do not know how I must do it. I cannot; I cannot do for myself. I am weak and you are strong, please do it for me.

How will I live my life, if you leave me alone? It is difficult for me to move around; when I see your absences. Sometimes I feel your absence and thought you have left me alone. I will make a mistake, if you leave me a moment. It is tough for me to go, when I feel your absence. Why have you forsake me; Lord? My enemies are all over, wanting to find fault on me.

I do not understand my weakness. I always wrong, when I want to do right. I cannot do for myself; unless you do for me. How can I dare, do for myself? Hold me please; I am weak.

When I am listening; I wrong, when I am writing I make mistake, when I am walking, I flop and find fault when I am looking.

Who will rescue me from this weakness? It is only you; Lord. Hold me; I am weak. I cannot; dare, walk alone, please, do not leave me.

It is not my fault, I do not understand; please hold me, I am weak. I cannot push; I do not know how to control myself. Please, hold me, I am weak.

I am fast to do wrong than good and wish flesh than the spirit. That is, my nature; I do not know why it is so with me? I consider nothing, unless I wrong in doing.

Please, hold me, I am weak. Your condition is not problem to God. Though, you are the worse sinner on the earth. His word to is come and let us reason together.

It is not late and your sin is ordinary before His grace. He can forgive the sin above sin, only if you will accept you're wrong and confess before Him. He is faithful to give all your sins and then cleanse you from it.

It does not matter your weakness or your sins that you been committed. God is able to forgive you by accepting and confess it to Him.

He will not leave you to struggle alone and will not hide His face from you. Only recognize Him as your Lord and savior.

He cares and mind than His apples of His eyes. You are dear to Him and will not forsake you. Be not afraid to come to Him. He is merciful to forgive your sins and then cleanse you from all unrighteousness. You cannot live by your strength.

You will fail and be as nothing. Do not allow perplexities overcome you. You I cannot; dare, control the forces around the globe. Only allow His to rule and guide.

Your life cannot be accepted by God. If you dare, live by your own strength. It is not you but it is Him who works in us to His good pressure and what pleases Him.

For by grace we have been saving, not by works, and then anyone should boast. You always need Christ to lead you. He is presence each minute to help and rescue sinners.

He is calling you with His tender voice; He is calling, He is calling, oh sinner come home. The beauty of His calling is that, He does not demand anything from you.

Your duty is to accept His voice and then go as He is calling you. Though, you are weak, but His grace is abundant for your weakness. Hold me; please, I am weak. Only accept it this way, He will accept you and then forgive you.

For Good Living; salvation and Knowledge Gain!
B. B. S. LIFE BOOKS.

You Are Glorified Page

Also by Bernard Benson Sarfo

The Fact Among Facts (1st)
The Fact Among Facts

Standalone
The Youth Murderer
Be Original Not a Copy
The Christians Science or Scholarship
Precious than Paradise
Habit Makes Future
A shelter from storm and rain
The Science of Life
The Strongest Lion Knockback
The Perfect and Inspiring City
Above Hope, Faith and Love
The Hero's Brave Decisions
The Weakest Among Plants
The Hero's Brave Decisions
Doing Above The Ability
The Wisdom Beyond Power And Greatness
Heavier Than the Heavens
The Academics Brains and Recreation Logics
The Strange Voice

The Chaotic World
Don't Miss Your Flight
Let the Nations Ponder
You Are Your Thoughts
I AM has sent me to you
Life Tools
The Fact Among Facts
You Are Glorified

About the Author

Bernard Benson Sarfo is an acquainted architectural designer and a motivational speaker.He is a gifted teacher who continues to motivate and encourage many.

Read more at https://www.amazon.com//author/bbslifebooks.

9 798224 422746